Silver Threads

Silver Threads

Poems

by Mary Howard

Small Batch Books

Amherst, Massachusetts

Cover and section openers designed by Christine Fogel

Cover image and interior photos by Mary Howard, with the
exception of page 21, photo by Ellen Cohen.

Interior design by Anny Wong

Library of Congress Control Number 2014960142
ISBN 978-1-937650-49-0

SMALL
BATCH
BOOKS

493 South Pleasant Street
Amherst, Massachusetts 01002
413.230.3943
smallbatchbooks.com

For Will

CONTENTS

Places

Corsica / 2

Tangier Island / 3

Clouds on Vieques / 4

San Miguel de Allende / 5

Kateland and Carolyn on Jacksonville Beach / 6

For Sale: 14 Atlantic Avenue, Vinalhaven / 7

Chinatown Fish / 8

Puerto Rican Men / 9

Naumkeag / 10

Long Island / 11

Love Songs

Love Song / 14

My Promise / 15

Night Walk; You Are / 16

Hibiscus / 17

Your Voice / 18

Something Wonderful; Insomnia / 19

I Love You / 20

Flying / 21

Time; Then and Now / 22

Artists

Robert Indiana / 24

Broken Obelisk / 25

Iceberg / 26

Christo / 27

The Violin / 28

Yo-Yo Ma / 29

Silver Threads

5:00 a.m.; Regret; The Hummingbird; Fall / 32

Irena's Sculpture Garden / 33

Vulnerable / 34

Ashes / 35

The Forest / 36

Jack / 37

Witness / 38

Leaves of Gold / 39

The World Inside / 40

Trees / 41

Snow / 42

Silver Threads / 43

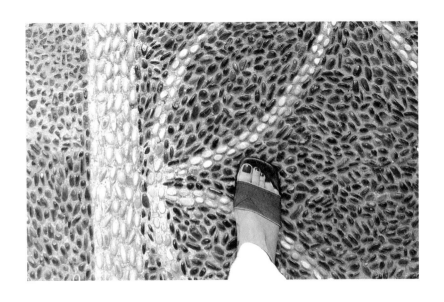

Places

Corsica

You watch from your protective enclave,
a mountain village high above the sea,
safe from many centuries of warriors
wanting to capture your island,
rape your wives and drink your wine.
Your fractured faces are as coarse as the earth—
red, the mountains rise with circuitous paths
around ravines that fall thousands of feet
only to rise again.
And so you are strong and loyal—
some say mafia—
but, of course,
you have learned from experience
the desperate price of freedom.
Quiet footsteps of the mountain goat,
wild pigs, an occasional horse,
your companions in the night,
not alone, but always awake,
watching for strangers
who do not belong.

Tangier Island

They are all there,
some dead, some alive—
Parks, Pruitt, Crockett—
on Tangier Island.
Golf carts on Long Bridge,
bicycles and deliveries from Lorraine's—
fried oyster sandwiches, crab cakes—
everybody smiles.
Swings with sagging seats
drift in the ocean breeze,
lazy day, school's out.
Fishing boats wander
in and out among the docks;
a six-year-old boy
sifts through the garbage
for spare parts to complete his toy barge.
His name is probably Parks
and his future bride, a Pruitt.
And so it goes, a continuous loop,
generation after generation.

Clouds on Vieques

Clouds,

round and white,

clustered in families,

sweeping over an island in emerald water,

occasionally filled with soft rain,

mostly moving gently,

east to west,

going somewhere at a happy pace,

Green Beach, maybe,

or to visit the wild horses

or to touch the noses

of the dogs sleeping in the street,

at night protecting the stars.

I can almost touch them

as they pass over the roof

and rest on the mountain,

then in an instant are gone.

San Miguel de Allende

The hill below me,
a megaphone,
pulses with sound, weaving around my ears,
my blood throbbing, wincing at each pass.
The sword will come next.

The wave of human conquest roars.
The bull, an innocent spectacle,
kneels in its own blood,
sighing at the feet
of the triumphant matador.

The ground of the stadium
lies red in the cool night,
darkness covers the deeds of the day,
while the joyous fall out into the street
celebrating the New Year.

Kateland and Carolyn on Jacksonville Beach

You weren't swimming exactly,
just flirting with the winter water
curving in and out of the edge,
where sand can be made into mud balls
and castle dreams rise and fall at the water's whim.

We walked forever miles—
crab legs, shells, a tree branch—
whatever looked like it would make the journey—
you flying like seagulls around my feet,
away across the water and back again,
only to be picked up by another gust
of excitement.

Sand-scratched knees and salt-knotted hair—
you gave in to the cool evening air,
starting toward the path,
looking back every few seconds,
making sure the water would still be there
when you return
tomorrow.

For Sale:
14 Atlantic Avenue, Vinalhaven

You are a house of the second empire,
your tower strong above your mansard roof—
weathered face, eyebrows on your windows.

Memories,
children at Christmas, my brother had chickenpox.
Ladybugs in jars collected from the roses,
iced tea on the porch, lemons, fresh-picked mint
sitting in bunches in the pitcher.

You withstood nor'easters,
snow, salt, wind, sun.
Your new owners
will only borrow you for a time.

Chinatown Fish

His gills open and close,
open and close,
tail still flapping
on the wood table,
ice drops clustered between
him and his brothers,
not dead but not of this world.
The proud merchant displays his wares—
he will fetch a good price,
he is still breathing,
his skin, translucent—
a touch of pink.
I can see him swimming
in schools through the seaweed.
There is a place he will go now,
not the home he once knew.
His gills open and close,
open and close,
his tail still flapping.

Puerto Rican Men

The music of the belly dancers
climbs into the air on the beach—
hips pounding, smooth bellies,
women in white, black hair waving
across their perfect backs,
rippling stomach muscles,
gold dangles dancing,
catching the reflections
of colored lights against palm trees
and the blue-green water of the pool.
Intoxicating rhythm,
waves frothing on the beach,
the night sky filling with fireworks—
sparkles, colors, a million shooting stars.
The men gather,
arm in arm,
drunk on too much rum,
hungry for sex
and the belly dancers,
swaying in one embrace, singing.
The sand moves in and out,
the beach receiving each lick,
the clock ticking toward midnight.

Naumkeag

Spirits rise, white tails waltzing among the birch trees,
cradling the walk of circles up the hill,
a trickle of water in the center of the path,
eyes in the windows looking down on fields of cows.
At night the fireflies light the tips of grasses,
winds caress the turret, glance across the roof.
All the while the spirits dance,
gloved hands twirling in the air.
Did the tree peonies bloom this year?
Sounds of the butler, children, afternoon tea, toast on a silver tray—
a memory, as gentle drops of rain fall into the ground,
moistening roots that grow taller trees.
When the season changes,
they must stand strong against the wintery winds
thrashing up the hill from the meadow,
threatening the house, sternly anchored to the mountain rock.
In spring, butterflies will return again to play among the flowers,
as if nothing ever happened,
but the spirits know,
and they will never tell.

Long Island

Three generations stringing beans,
I am the one in between.

Nimble fingers familiar to each other's hands,
the curl of the knife slicing the long way,
quiet sharing, hopes, dreams, and memories,
last night's laughter resonating in our eyes,
the warmth of the radiator making our cheeks glow.
Dogs, guitars, and the football game always on—
no one really watching but welcoming the familiar sound,
the stadium filled, the hum of the crowd.
This is your family, and mine now too,
turkey, pierogi, and cranberry sauce,
how fine the twine that binds us close
at each task, setting, lighting, basting, prayers, and toasts.

Three generations stringing beans,
I am the one in between.

Love Songs

Love Song

A lone white horse pauses at the edge of the beach,

dark eyes search my soul.

Are you ready to ride?

Will you trust the journey?

Hold firm to my back through the twists in the path,

the dark of the past, the unknown approach to the shore.

Slide your hands across my neck,

feel my muscles carrying us so far.

And when the gate welcomes us

to that place beyond time,

will you ride through with me fearless,

but not alone, simply with the pain of two

becoming one?

My Promise

No one will ever know
    what I write for you
        and what I write for me.

Words turn in flocks,
    a thousand metaphors set to flight
        on the wings of birds passing before the sun,
            casting shadows on my page.

No one will ever know your name
    or know your gentle spirit as I know it,
        except as I spin you in my thoughts
            and weave my dreams through the curls of your hair.

Quiet the eagle stands,
    proud on the rock, a beautiful nose,
        his wisdom beyond all time,
            forever anonymous.

Even as the sun sets beyond the apple tree
    I will not shine my light on your face
        or call your name to the wind.
            You will always remain
              unspoken.

Night Walk

Save time for me
when the moon is a wisp of feather,
to walk on tree light patterns,
crunch the autumn leaves,
and hold my hand forever.

You Are

You Are
the blue space between the clouds,
the whisper of wind between the stars,
the silence between the dog's bark,
the pause before the first note.

Hibiscus

Let's leave
for the cloud on the island peak,
where we can retrieve
the love we hid so long ago.
Sit by my side,
smile in the clean air,
and I'll write you a poem.
We'll share a moment,
away from the noise,
and open like the hibiscus
to the morning light—
delicate, wet with dew—
feeling the history
of the many times
we have seen the flower
but never felt its petals—
fragile, defenseless, but ready.

Your Voice

Finally, your voice.
I can almost touch you.
I want to tell you about the white curtain
blowing in my bedroom,
the ocean waves in my ear,
the changes in each sunset
and how much I want you near.
Don't hurry now,
wait,
hold me with your voice,
smooth like your hands.
I need you with me in this quiet place
so I can love you. I miss your face.
Your voice is deep.
I feel you under the sheets
and in the shower.
I miss you hour by hour.

Something Wonderful

When you were born,
the moon passed in front of the sun;
the eclipse was a celestial event.
In that moment of darkness,
a thousand stars were born in your heart,
a million soft breaths on your face,
a billion galaxies in your eyes.
Having you as my son
is the best, most profound
something wonderful found.

Insomnia

For you
life has been half a bed of nails.
So many restless nights
leave you sad and lonely.
If only you could see
the other half—
that life is half a bed of roses—
you could take in the
deep red of the flower
and lay on its soft petals
until darkness and quiet
enter your body,
cushioned by a bed of magic.

I Love You

I love you in the morning,
I love you in the night,
I love you in the flowers,
and in a thousand starry skies.

I love you when the day is starting,
I love you when night is drawing nigh,
I love you in dreamy passages,
as time is passing by.

I feel the breath between us,
lips exchanging souls,
arms wrapped around us,
whispers in the cold.

When our time is over,
I will let you go.
I will never forget the passion
when you held me close.

I love you in the morning,
I love you in the night,
I love you in the flowers,
and in a thousand starry skies.

Flying

I will never look at a cloud
the same way again,
nor the sky, nor the water's edge.
High above the earth,
a single prop turns
on super cub 55 papa zulu.
Your arms guide a simple stick,
escaping all boundaries,
below us the cliffs of the Bay of Fundy,
whales playing outside its walls,
tides filling high when they are in.
Our spirits absorb the safety of sunlight,
my hands touch your sides.
In a round mirror, your gentle smile,
I trust you with my life.
I will never look at a cloud
the same way again.

Time

how do we slow the process   *time*

each minute suspended then   *stops*

listen to our hearts, souls, thoughts   *whisper*

silence. in you. in me. gifts.   *quietly*

while we tumble, hide, hold   *in love*

passing slowly, the night, the morning   *together*

Then and Now

I didn't recognize the line
between then and now,
when then stopped and now began.
All my senses said there is no line.
But when you died, I discovered
then and now.

Artists

Robert Indiana

in Vinalhaven, Maine

So, Mr. Indiana—
you do flags
and stars and LOVE
in repetition, usually separate.

Your eyes twinkle.
I like your hat with the flaps turned up.

You dream in the middle of the night
when images tease your mind.
Maybe it is the repetition—
I repeat myself, therefore I am—

that causes you, Mr. Indiana, to do flags
and stars and LOVE.

Broken Obelisk

after Barnett Newman in the MoMA Sculpture Garden

The broken obelisk,

inverted on a pyramid,

intersecting in a sacred place

of harmony,

teetering

on a single point of balance.

A slight breath of air

could send it all into chaos.

We stay in that state,

hoping the wind won't change,

holding each other in the black of night,

knowing uncertainty might shake our dreams.

Iceberg

after William Bradford's painting of the Arctic

Men feel so small, standing before
your immense white—
frozen—
a giant Parthenon,
built by an ethereal hand,
lifting from the sea.

An arched opening to see through
to another world,
where tall-masted schooners
surrender white sails
to the force of the wind,
cold on the face of those
seeking to find the other side.

Christo

in Central Park, New York

orange gate

orange gate

orange gate

symbol of civilization

imposed on a landscape of change

billows of children's laughter moving

       around and through

           around and through

orange fabric waving

in winds of thought

centuries of processions

while orderly adults adhere to the path

an unconscious celebration of myths

and a human need for belonging

The Violin

based on a composition by Jakov Jakoulov for the violinist Alexandre Jakoulov

A lone voice,
the single string of a violin
calls in the cold night.
In the distance, the wind whispers in solitude,
echoing the crystal mist of breath.

The moon, silver in the cobalt sky,
watches as the orphaned children sleep.

A lone voice calls in the cold night,
delicate pitch, yearning for a response.
The trees bend to hear more closely.
In near silence, the crackling leaves
heave a desperate sigh.

In the darkest hours before the dawn,
a shooting star lights the endless sky,
passing overhead, leaving other stars behind,
emerging with hope for daylight
and a galaxy of comforting hands.

But in the gulag, the only voice
is one note on the gypsy violin,
calling in the cold night.

Yo-Yo Ma

plays "Pickin'" by John Williams at Tanglewood

This disconnected music was created for you to play,
many notes but no melody,
chords with no sequence,
high low
left right
up down.
Your cello, round between your legs,
waited three hundred years for this night.

Rocking gently,
eyes closed,
brilliance travels through your hands,
resonates through your body
as we sit, humbly
in awe of the magic you create.
Your cello sings
and fireflies dance in the Berkshire air.

Silver Threads

5:00 a.m.

The leaves and grass are intensely green.
They have taken a bath and
are waiting for the morning sun
to dry them with a towel of light.

Regret

The missed rainbow
takes joy away
from the celebration
of the first crocus.

The Hummingbird

Quiet, the hummingbird sits on the porch rail.
It is you,
I see you in its eyes.
Across the bay a loon calls to his mate,
a lonely, distant sound,

I am here, are you there?

Fall

Leaves land
with a sigh
on the brown earth.

Irena's Sculpture Garden

Full—always full.
Green, yellow, violet, crimson.
Faces on lacquered bodies—
not quite scary,
not quite beautiful. Round.
Vines gather, a wedding dress
drawn to the neck of one face,
feminine,
inviting things to grow on her trellises—
tomatoes, beans.

Each week a new flower,
new flower, new flower.
Roses everywhere—
some for me to take home.
Now a nosegay of herbs—
rosemary, parsley, oregano.
Growing closer every day.
Friendship
is always full
in Irena's garden.

Vulnerable

Standing tall,

the coreopsis

before the hail came,

ice pellets on yellow flowers,

stinging.

Winds of satanic level

breaking stems.

All of your majesty bows

to the air you once trusted.

The sun hides its eyes behind black clouds,

lightning, electric spears.

So violent,

so desolate

and yet,

so irresistible.

Ashes

So here you are—
ashes, bones, cinder.
Your warmth passed through my fingers,
transporting you to the next place—
some of you in Gardiners Bay,
some in a small jar in Stockbridge,
scattered—
waiting for me to join you,
which I will one day
and then I too will be
ashes, bones, cinder
settling on the green grass
under the black metal cross.

The Forest

I have been to the center
      of the forest alone.
There I saw a sapling
      and the vastness of the universe.
I felt its darkness with a shudder
      and the fragments of light with relief.
I have been pricked by pine needles
      and touched by the softness of moss.
I have been awakened by the roar of the bear
      and heard the silence of the snow.

Jack

and so you slipped away
past the row of daffodils,
across the tall grasses of the field,
up Maple Hill,
beyond the Big Dipper,
the dust of Hale-Bopp
and the clouds of the Milky Way,
to places we have never been.

Witness

It was a calm day
as the seagulls waved gently,
white against the blue sky,
the delicacy of the moment,
the balance of time that has no time,
the record that exists only in my eyes.

The smaller seagull swooped
once, twice.
His rhythm wasn't smooth,
young brown feathers beating
against fear.

The older gulls began grouping high above
and in flocks with a mission.
They attacked,
attacked,
attacked.

His wings lay deflated at the water's edge.
He went to that place where seagull souls go alone,
feathers in the wind and bones reduced to sand,
drifting with the water
to the end of the horizon.

I was horrified, yet honored, to have been
his witness.

Leaves of Gold

More gold in sunshine, piles of coins,
waiting for the wind to pick them up.
Dancing in circles higher,
gathering in a swirling cone,
reaching for the clouds,
moving faster than in the soft air of summer.
Running across the sky before the cold of winter
pushes them back to Earth.
They will lay hard against the ground,
dancing, but a memory.

The World Inside

The eye of a hurricane is a quiet place.

Outside fury spins away from its center,
the chaos of waves and wind gathers strength,
pummeling the shore in a nasty rage.

But the eye is still,
the air sweet, calm, and gentle—
a haven of child's breath.

This is the world inside,
a place where danger is not
and I am free.

Trees

Let's get naked.
Shed our colors—yellow, red, brown—
and find our arms free
to wave about in the wind.

Let's find room between us.
Let's shout to the mountain,
"We're ready to start
our sleeping time."

It's quiet now, just the hush of cold.
My skin is thick, my veins empty.
My arms reach toward you
until we almost touch.

Together we pray
for spring.

Snow

The air, filled with white,

frozen swirls in the wind with my crystal brothers,

wandering across, up, down, sideways,

white goose down feathers

with no particular place to be, free

from the schedule of the day, the hands of the clock,

the bill to be paid, the apology to be made.

I unfold my soul like a blanket,

lying on the cold brown earth,

facing the sky, holding its endless patterns

in my eyes, melting

with the first warm rays of spring.

Soon I will be part of the river—

my journey will change,

my destination: the sea.

Silver Threads

A thin line on the horizon,

lying between deep blue and rose,

wraps the Earth in a silver thread,

giving pause to the tick of time,

providing a brief moment of celebration

before the pull of night.

In all things living and not—

in mothers, sons, and lovers,

trees, flowers, snowflakes—

a single thread becomes many,

and many become many more.

You are my thread, and I, yours,

always.

That is my promise.

Poet Mary Howard grew up in Boston but spent summers living in a stone mill in West Stockbridge, Massachusetts. There, her father taught her how to fish and throw a machete; her brother, how to climb trees; and her grandmother, how to write a poem every night before bed. Thus began a lifelong passion for the natural world and for poetry. Even when she and her late husband, Bob Charczuk, ran an architectural design firm in New York, they returned to the Berkshires on weekends with their son, Will.

Many walks in the woods and much travel in the world beyond inspired the images and feelings in this book, her first collection of poems and photographs. Mary Howard continues to divide her time between New York City and the Berkshires.

CPSIA information can be obtained at www.ICGtesting.com
Printed in the USA
LVIW01n0948080415
433748LV00001B/1

* 9 7 8 1 9 3 7 6 5 0 4 9 0 *